Prehistoric Animals

Copyright © 1988, Raintree Publishers Inc.

Translated by Hess-Inglin Translation Services

Library of Congress Number: 87-28713

1 2 3 4 5 6 7 8 9 0   91 90 89 88 87

Printed and bound in the United States of America.

Library of Congress Cataloging in Publication Data

Prehistoric Animals.

   (Science and its secrets)
   Includes index.
   Summary: An introduction to the first animal life on earth, describing fossils, reptiles that ruled the world in the age of dinosaurs, and early mammals.
      1. Paleontology—Juvenile literature.   [1. Paleontology.
2. Prehistoric animals]   I. Series.
QE714.5.P75   1988   560—dc19   87-28713
ISBN 0-8172-3082-3 (lib. bdg.)
ISBN 0-8172-3088-2 (softcover)

PREHISTORIC ANIMALS

🌳 Raintree Publishers — Milwaukee

Contents

The reign of the dinosaurs

The rise of mammals

FOSSILS

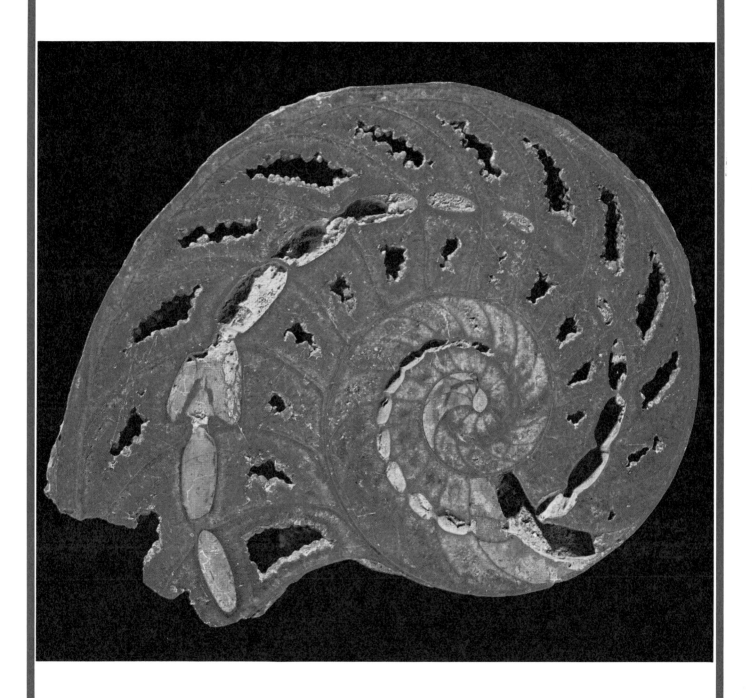

What is a fossil?

A fossil is the remains of a plant or animal that lived in the past. Everything known about animals and plants that no longer exist today has been revealed through the study of fossils.

Perhaps you have seen small shellfish in layers of sand or the imprint of shellfish in blocks of limestone or sandstone. These rocks were formed a very long time ago at the bottom of lakes and seas. These bodies of water have now dried up.

While these rocks were still muddy, they trapped the creatures that populated these waters. After an animal dies, its body is usually destroyed. But sometimes it is quickly

Fossils as well preserved as this fish are rare. In this very fine-grained rock, even some soft parts have left their imprint.

In these drawings, you can see the various stages in the fossilization of a fish.

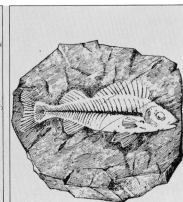

buried in mud or sand. Then its hardest parts may be preserved.

This is why many animals found in the fossil state are those that lived in water. Land animals have less chance of becoming fossils. Their bodies are exposed to scavengers, rain, and wind for a long time. However, they are sometimes carried off by a stream of water. Then they are preserved in its silt. On solid ground, they are sometimes buried under volcanic ash, under dust carried by the wind, or in the clay in a cave.

So, buried for million of years, shells and bones undergo changes as the rock surrounding them hardens. Under certain conditions, people have been lucky enough to find traces of soft parts, such as skin, feathers, or fur. Plants can be fossilized, too.

There are some very unusual cases of fossilization. Whole, huge mammoths have been found frozen in the icy soil of Siberia. Their flesh was so well preserved that the dogs of the explorers who had discovered them were able to eat it. Another remarkable example is that of insects encased in amber on the shores of the Baltic Sea. This beautiful yellow substance that is used in jewelry is, in fact, a fossil resin of conifer trees. It is nearly forty million years old. Some fossils represent traces of the activities of extinct creatures. For example, animal footprints are sometimes found in slabs of rock. These are evidence of the passage of animals over a muddy surface, which has since hardened.

Paleontologists (scientists who study fossils) even work under water! A skeleton of a mammoth has been discovered in a flooded cave in Florida.

This insect was imprisoned in resin forty million years ago. This substance was transformed into amber, and it has preserved the finest details of the animal's anatomy.

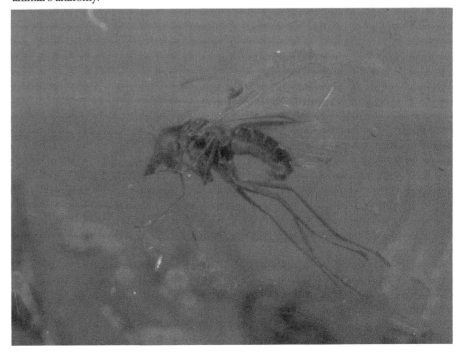

9

In the field, the paleontologist carefully uses large tools when necessary. Here, the hammer allows him to remove the shoulder blade of a dinosaur from very hard rock.

On the other hand, in the laboratory, the work calls for great attention to detail. Very fine tools and chemicals are important.

Where and how are fossils found?

There are fossils in a great many areas of the world. All sedimentary rocks, deposited under water or on the ground, can contain them. Often, the discovery of animal or plant fossils happens by accident while digging the foundation for a house or building a highway. When geologists study a region, they gather all the fossils that they find because the study of them provides important information about the past.

On the basis of this information, paleontologists organize expeditions to discover and study the most interesting groups of fossils.

Extracting fossils is sometimes easy. For example, fossils such as solid shells are sometimes found in soft clay or sandstone. But it can also be very difficult. When the rock is hard and the fossil is fragile, special techniques must be used.

Have living creatures changed with time?

The animals and plants of the world never seem to change. In reality, this is not true. Over the last million years, many species, or kinds, of living things have changed. Some have been totally replaced. Fossils are evidence of this. They show creatures that were ancestors of today's animals and plants.

One of the best examples of this is *archaeopteryx*. This bird is the most ancient bird known. It still has many characteristics of its ancestors, the reptiles. For instance, it has teeth on its jaws. Fossils like these show how one animal group gave birth to another. They fill the gaps between countless living creatures of today's world. In some cases, fossils have made it possible to trace a creature's development. Then a paleontologist can reassemble the stages between an early creature and its modern version. The history of the horse has been traced this way. Its ancestors are nearly 50 million years old.

These reconstructions also show that evolution rarely follows a straight line. Evolution is the process by which organisms slowly change. Most often, the "family trees" of animal or plant groups have many branches. The study of fossils has also uncovered certain rules of evolution. For example, scientists now know that things almost never go in reverse. Once an organism is extinct, it will never reappear. Also, the same changes sometimes occur in groups that are different but live in the same way. For example, the *ichthyosaurs* are reptiles which adopted the appearance of fish. This is called a convergence. Studying modern living creatures can explain the evolution of a species. But only the science of fossils, or paleontology, can retrace the path of this evolution.

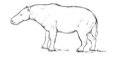

The brontotheres are distant cousins of horses and rhinoceroses. In this case, evolution resulted in a great increase in size. Also note the spectacular development of the horns.

The first scientists who defended the theories of evolution were greatly criticized. Charles Darwin, especially, was often ridiculed. Here he is shown with an ape's body.

How is an extinct animal reconstructed?

With each discovery, reconstructions of extinct animals come closer to reality. The iguanodon *(above)* was drawn in the nineteenth century based on a few small parts. The replica *(below)* was reconstructed using a complete skeleton. Originally the iguanodon was thought to have a horn. This horn turned out to be a spur on its thumb.

Some extinct animals, such as shellfish, look like those living today. So it is easy to know what they looked like when they were alive. But others are nothing like today's animals. In this case, the work is much more difficult.

Take vertebrates, for example. Vertebrates are animals having backbones. With these animals, reconstruction is often started with only some of the bones. The shape, or anatomy, of today's animals are used to help. Then the scientist tries to understand how the muscles were attached to the skeleton. How the skin covered it is also considered. But the paleontologist must guess at many of the details. Because of this guesswork, reconstructions of the same animal sometimes look very different.

How long have people been looking for fossils?

Even prehistoric people gathered shellfish fossils that looked strange or pretty. Fossils have been found in their caves. In ancient times, Greek scholars studied the fossils of sea animals. They thought that fossils of sea animals must have formed in the sea. Therefore, land where fossils were found must have once been under water. But for a long time, the origin of fossils was debated. Some people thought they came from a mysterious force within the earth. Others saw them as the devil's work.

In time, it became clear that fossils were the remains of animals or plants that had lived a long time ago. At the end of the eighteenth century, the science of fossils, paleontology, was developed. It was begun in Europe by scientists like Baron Cuvier. Cuvier studied the fossils of vertebrates. From his studies, he made drawings of early animals. Since then, paleontology has spread over the whole world.

The scene is the United States in the beginning of the nineteenth century. Paleontologists are already hard at work. Many workers are excavating, or digging up, the bones of a mastodon. A machine in the center empties water from the hole.

How are fossils dated?

The living world evolved over time. The fossils formed in one period are different from older or more recent ones. Paleontologists can trace the sequence of fossil groupings that characterize each period. When a fossil is found, it is placed in this sequence. Paleontologists are then able to date it in relation to the events of the earth and life. Also, they have physical means of dating rocks and sometimes fossils. They have now prepared a "calendar" which establishes the approximate age of all discoveries.

Today, chemical and physical methods of dating fossils have been added to field work. These methods sometimes require costly and complex equipment.

What is a living fossil?

Fossils can give a true "photograph" of extinct animals. The 140 million years between these two horseshoe crabs have hardly changed the animal at all. The horseshoe crab is a good example of a living fossil.

A "living fossil" is an animal or plant that has not changed much since very ancient times. The horseshoe crab is an example. It is still found on the coasts of America. This animal has hardly changed for 200 million years. Sometimes creatures like this are first found as fossils. Later they are discovered in their present-day form. This was the case with the famous *coelacanth,* a fish found in fossil form. It was believed to have become extinct 65 million years ago. But living specimens, caught between Africa and the island of Madagascar, disproved this.

Are there fake fossils?

Extinct creatures have interested people for a long time. Some people even went so far as to make fake fossils. Sometimes these were nothing but the remains of genuine animals. In the nineteenth century, a certain Doctor Koch traveled throughout America and England showing a "sea serpent." The fossil turned out to be the vertebrae of several whales.

Some fakes were much cruder. In the eighteenth century, a Professor Beringer, at the University of Würzburg, Germany, became the victim of his students' joke. The students constructed several sculptures. They made the professor think that the fossils were real.

But the most famous case is that of the "Piltdown man." The Piltdown man was found in England in 1912. Forty years later, the experts realized the fossil was a fake. A clever forger had made it by using a human skull and an ape's jaw.

THE START OF LIFE

How did life start on the earth?

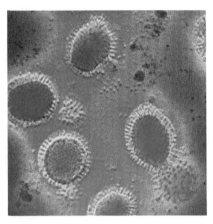

Viruses are very simple organisms. Early life forms must have been very like them.

The earth began as a ball of molten matter. About 4½ billion years ago, it started to cool. Its crust then grew solid, but the core was still very hot. At this point, the atmosphere had very little oxygen in it. It was made mainly of hydrogen, methane, ammonia, and water vapor. As the earth cooled even further, the water vapor changed to liquid. Floods of rain poured down upon barely cooled lava. Little by little, the first oceans formed.

Even after the oceans formed, it was a long time before life started. The atmosphere continued to be ravaged by intense heat and radiation from the sun. Until a protective layer called ozone could develop, the earth's surface could not support life. But chemists think that these very conditions set off chemical reactions in the ocean. Certain chemicals came together under just the right conditions and formed microscopic globules. These single-celled creatures became more and more complicated. At some point, these creatures took on the characteristics of life. They were able to take in food. They grew and divided. Today's disease viruses are a good example of these early life forms.

Some rocks found in coastal waters contain many fossils. These fossils are evidence of the many life forms that the early oceans supported. The ocean conditions of the time were very favorable.

How did life begin on land?

The radiation that bombarded the earth began life in the oceans. But these same rays, and specifically ultraviolet rays, were also deadly. Any creature that left the protection of the water was in danger. In the oceans, new life forms were multiplying. But the land that had emerged stayed deserted for a long time.

Over time, oxygen collected in the atmosphere. Much of this oxygen was made by plants. High in the atmosphere, this oxygen formed a gas called ozone. The ozone formed a layer around the earth that protected it from harmful ultraviolet rays. Finally the land became bearable. Only then could plants and animals leave the sea to live on the land.

This ozone layer took hundreds of millions of years to develop. Before this, life on earth was slow to develop. Once enough oxygen had developed, however, life began to grow and change very quickly.

Twenty thousand years ago, Europe was an icy landscape. Reindeer herds like this one traveled as far south as northern Spain. Ten thousand years ago, the climate warmed. Europe then began to look much like it does today.

Has the earth always looked the same?

Microscopic creatures were the only life forms for millions of years. Very early, these creatures divided into two major groups. The first groups (early animals) lived off of the second group (early plants). To survive, the early plants learned to live off of a very simple substance: carbon dioxide. With sunlight, this gas was changed to a food source. In this way, animals and plants could thrive and co-exist.

The first plants in the oceans had an important role in the earth's history. They produced much of the atmosphere's oxygen. This gas—the very key to life—was made by life itself.

After that, the earth began to look more and more like it does today. But, climates and geography continued to change for hundreds of millions of years. The continents constantly moved about each other. They were even sometimes partly covered by shallow seas. This was the case in what is now Paris, France. Millions of years ago, this land was home to sponges and sea urchins. Today, paleontologists study fossils to learn more about an area's past.

Trilobites are among the most ancient fossilized animals. They are found in abundance. Their jointed shells make them similar to lobsters and crabs. The oldest date back more than 500 million years.

Where are the oldest traces of living creatures found?

A trilobite coiled back upon itself.

As the earth changed, mud on the ocean bottoms hardened into rock. Often, it formed around the remains of living creatures. As more layers formed, the mud was buried at greater and greater depths. There it was subject to higher temperatures and pressures. This compressed the mud, changing its structure considerably. Little by little the fossils in it were destroyed. In the end, many disappeared completely. This is why fossils older than 600 million years are rare.

The first living creatures were very small and very simple. They had no skeleton or shell. It was very difficult for them to become fossils. The oldest fossils are the one-celled plants such as algae or bacteria. Except for these, it is uncommon to find fossils formed before the Paleozoic era. The Paleozoic era began

600 million years ago.

The first spectacular fossil animals are those from Ediacara, Australia. They lived just before the start of the Paleozoic era. These animals had a fairly complex structure. They included jellyfish, worms, soft corals, and other strange creatures. They were the result of a long evolution which remains a mystery. Their preservation is unique. None of these animals had hard parts.

Finally, about 600 million years ago, plants and animals developed skeletons and shells. This helped them spread over the entire planet. In the beginning of the Paleozoic era, these sea creatures began to leave their remains in rocks. These included tiny shell creatures, sponges, and corals. Others such as crustaceans with jointed shells and sea urchins are also found in early fossils.

FROM THE SEA
TO SOLID GROUND

What did the first vertebrates look like?

Lampreys are fish with no jaws. The first vertebrates probably looked something like them.

Vertebrates are animals with backbones. Specifically, vertebrates have bodies supported by an internal skeleton with jointed parts. These skeletons are made of bone or cartilage. The oldest known bone chips are about 500 million years old.

Early in the Paleozoic era, the only vertebrates were primitive fish with jawless mouths. The jawless fish lived alongside more modern animals for a long time. Its skeleton was made mostly of cartilage. It also had bony plates which formed a shield around its head and thorax. Some fish had uneven fins and probably swam awkwardly. Such a fish balanced itself using long bony spines on its sides. Others were more highly evolved. They had true fins.

These jawless fish ate only small particles. These particles entered the fish's mouth along with the water used for breathing. Once the water had irrigated its gills, it went out through openings on either side of its head.

Did the first fish have enemies?

In the time of jawless fish, there were other strange animals. One looked something like today's scorpions. This "water scorpion" is placed beside jawless fish in most scientific classifications. Scientific classification is a method of identifying and organizing living things.

The water scorpion was a monstrous animal. It grew to be 6 feet (2 meters) long. It had powerful claws at the ends of its jointed arms. These were probably used to grab small jawless fish and eat them. The bony shell of the jawless fish probably protected it from such attacks.

A nineteenth century English cartoon shows the eurypterid or giant water scorpion. Eurypterids were already attracting public attention at this early date.

Survivors

The lamprey and the myxine are survivors of the jawless fish. Both are parasites. Parasites are organisms that depend on others' help to survive, but give nothing in return. These fish use their teeth to attach themselves to other fish. They then feed on the other animals' bodies.

20

How did fish with jaws appear?

Over time, the bony arches supporting the jawless fish's gills began to change. This change caused the fish to develop true jaws. This was very important. Fish with jaws were able to swallow large prey. They no longer had to live on fine particles or live as parasites.

The oldest vertebrates with jaws were small fish with fins supported by bony spines. In the Devonian period, many other forms appeared. Heavily armored fish called *placoderms* were one type. These sometimes grew to be 21 feet (6 m) long. Some of these were fearsome carnivores, or meat eaters. The first sharks also appeared during this time. Finally, the "bony fish" appeared. These fish were named for their well-developed skeletons.

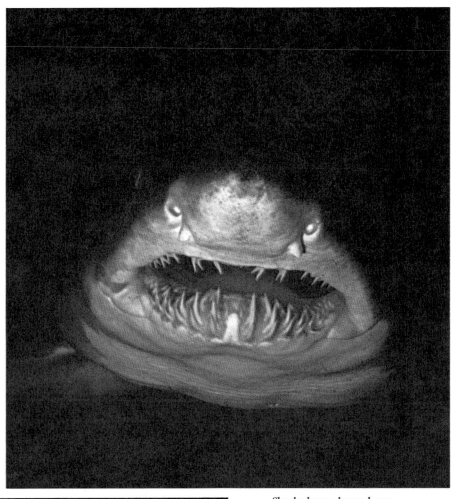

Sharks have always been remarkably adaptable animals. An animal that adapts can adjust to new environments or situations. These carnivores have never had any real competitors. Even today, they are a thriving group. Over the years, they have not changed much.

The many teeth of a shark are constantly replaced. Because of this, they are found fossilized in many rocks.

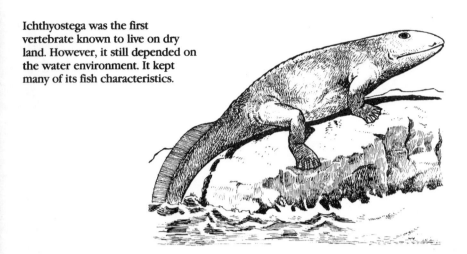

Ichthyostega was the first vertebrate known to live on dry land. However, it still depended on the water environment. It kept many of its fish characteristics.

What were the first animals to live on land?

Plants were the first to thrive on land 400 million years ago. As the world became favorable, animals soon followed them. The first animals were creatures related to centipedes. These were followed by spiders and insects. These animals had no internal skeleton. Hard shells protected these animals and supported their bodies out of the water. They even learned to breathe the atmosphere's oxygen. For this, they developed a system of branched tubes. These tubes ran through their entire bodies and linked with the outside.

Before long, vertebrates also moved into this new environment. They adapted themselves by other means. They represented the second largest group of land animals.

Which was the largest insect?

By the end of the Paleozoic era, centipedes, spiders, and especially insects had developed a great deal. They thrived in the earth's warm and humid climate.

Plants also did well under these conditions. Huge forests covered great areas. There, ferns and horsetails grew as big as trees. As these plants died, they formed beds of plant debris. These rotting masses eventually formed huge coal beds. But in the meantime, they were an easy food source for the animals.

Under these conditions, the insects multiplied quickly. Some grew to surprising sizes. *Arthropleura,* a type of giant centipede, was almost 3 feet (1 m) long. The still-clumsy vertebrates were no real threat to these insects. This was especially true since no vertebrates could fly.

So, the insects were the masters of the air. One of them, called *Meganeura,* was a huge dragonfly. With its 16-inch (41 centimeter) wingspan, it ruled the swamps.

Great forests of ferns and plants thrived toward the end of the Paleozoic era. During this time, which is also known as the Carboniferous period, coal was formed. This was also an important time for insects. They reigned as masters of the air. Meganeura was the most impressive of all. This giant dragonfly was found fossilized in the coal mines of central France.

How did fish begin to leave the water?

Footprints in the mud become permanent records when the mud hardens into rock. Such records offer details about the presence of vertebrates on dry land. Such prints are often more abundant than bones. But they are sometimes more mysterious.

About 350 million years ago, "bony fish" lived in lagoons and ponds. Many of these water bodies dried up in the dry season. Whenever this happened, the fish with gills died. Their gills only allowed them to breathe in the water. However, some fish also developed lungs. With lungs, the fish could breathe the air. They could survive without water. Many of these fish had strong fins which they used to crawl awkwardly to other pools. Once out of the water, they found new sources of food. They then spent more and more time on dry land. Eventually, they adapted to this new environment. Slowly, these animals began to change. They became amphibians. Amphibians are animals that can live both in the open air and in the water.

Do lungfish still exist?

The lungfish can breathe in both the air and the water. In certain tropical regions there are still relatives of these fish. These are the dipnoans. These fish are also able to breathe just as well in the water as in the air. One of them, the *neoceratodus,* is found in Australia. This fish uses its lung to survive during the dry season. During that time, there is not much oxygen in the water. The two others are *protopterus* in Africa and *lepidosiren* in South America. In the dry period, these fish shut themselves up in holes. There they quietly wait for the rains to return. Fossils of the dipnoans' holes have been found in North America. This shows that this behavior is ancient.

The dipnoans are fish with lungs. They can breathe in the water or in the air. Relatives of these fish exist even today. This fish, the neoceratodus from the rivers of Australia, is one of these lungfish.

Today's amphibians, like their ancestors, go through a great process of physical change. This process, called metamorphosis, changes a tadpole into an adult frog such as this one.

Why did the first land animals stay close to the water?

At first, vertebrates that learned to live on dry land stayed close to the water. In fact, they dried out quickly if they did not wet themselves often. Their skin was bare like the skin of present-day frogs. It could not hold moisture in. Even more important, they had to lay their eggs in the water. This is where their tadpoles, which used gills to breathe, started to grow. Eventually, they would turn into adults with lungs. The oldest amphibians, like *ichthyostega,* spent much time in the water. This amphibian even had a fin on its tail, just like a fish's tail.

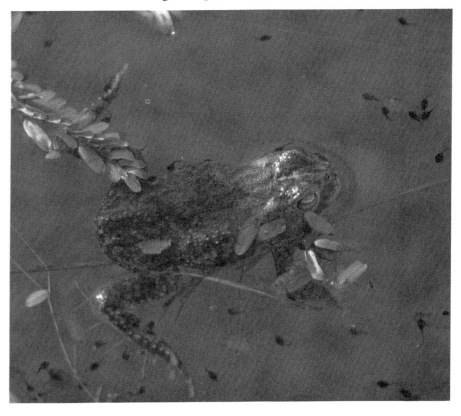

What animals lived at the time coal was formed?

The Paleozoic era's warm and humid climate encouraged the growth of huge forests. Their remains, constantly covered by layers of sand, were forced deep into the earth. Little by little, these layers of matter were transformed into veins of coal.

The remains of the first reptiles were discovered in the fossilized trunks of giant trees.

About 300 million years ago, there were many huge, swampy forests. They grew in many parts of the world. As they died and became fossilized, these forests formed coal.

Many animals lived in these forests. Insects, such as dragonflies and beetles, flew through the air or crawled on the ground. Some of these were monstrous in size. In the water, many fish evolved. These included strange freshwater sharks. Amphibians existed then in a variety of forms. Some were long like eels. Others looked more like salamanders and spent time in the water and on the land. The first reptiles were small and agile. They were able to spend their entire lives on dry land.

THE REPTILES
CONQUER THE WORLD

How did reptiles free themselves from the water environment?

This gavial has just hatched. The gavial is a reptile much like a crocodile, which still exists. The reptiles' success is partly due to their eggs. As they adapted to the land, their eggs developed a protective shell. This made reproduction outside of the water possible.

As bony fish adapted to the land, they developed lungs and limbs. But to free themselves of the water for good, they had much more changing to do.

To hear in the air, the amphibians developed a different kind of ear. The new ear was closed by a tight membrane, called the ear drum. It developed a system of bones that carried vibrations to the inner ear. The skin also had to change. It developed a soft, resistant layer of dead cells. This kept the animal from drying up and gave it additional protection. Their eyes now produced tears to keep them moist.

As the first reptiles appeared, the continents became populated. These animals laid eggs protected by a solid shell. In these eggs were nutrients for the embryo (developing animal). A separate, liquid-filled pocket gave the embryo room to grow. A third sac held its wastes.

These land vertebrates no longer returned to the water to reproduce. They no longer gave birth to tadpoles with gills. Instead, their young were able to live on solid ground.

What did the primitive reptiles become?

The first reptiles appeared as the large beds of coal were forming. That was about 300 million years ago. They did well where fish, amphibians, and insects were easy to find. These gave the reptiles an endless food source. As they thrived, they also took on varied forms. Some grew to amazing sizes. The *ophiacodons,* which fed on fish, looked like large iguanas. Some of their relatives had strange sail-like fins on their backs.

For example, there was *dimetrodon.* This reptile lived in North America toward the end of the Paleozoic era. It was about 13 feet (4 m) long. These reptiles probably used their large fins to control their body temperatures. When it was very hot, the many blood vessels in the fin released body heat. This helped the reptile's body cool down. But when the weather was cool, the fin helped absorb the sun's heat. The animal simply moved into the sun, and its blood warmed quickly. So dimetrodon was much more active than other reptiles that did

not have this organ. Dimetrodon was a meat-eater, or a carnivore. In this case, its fin gave it a big advantage over most of its prey. However, some herbivores, or plant-eaters, had a similar system.

At the start of the Mesozoic era, other groups of reptiles appeared. They developed alongside this group of reptiles with regulated body temperatures. Some of them disappeared fairly quickly. The heavy-set herbivore *pareiosaurus* is one example. This was also the case with the order of reptiles known as *mesosaurs.* Fossils of these animals have been discovered in South Africa and Brazil.

Other reptiles had a more glorious fate. One large order of reptiles was known as thecodonts. These reptiles had strong, pointed teeth and strong legs for running. During the Triassic period, the species within this order grew very different from one another. This order included ancestors of the dinosaurs and the crocodiles.

As the Paleozoic era closed, reptiles dominated the world. Dimetrodon, with its large dorsal fin, is one of the most well-known. During the Mesozoic era, these animals disappeared. Dinosaurs then ruled the earth.

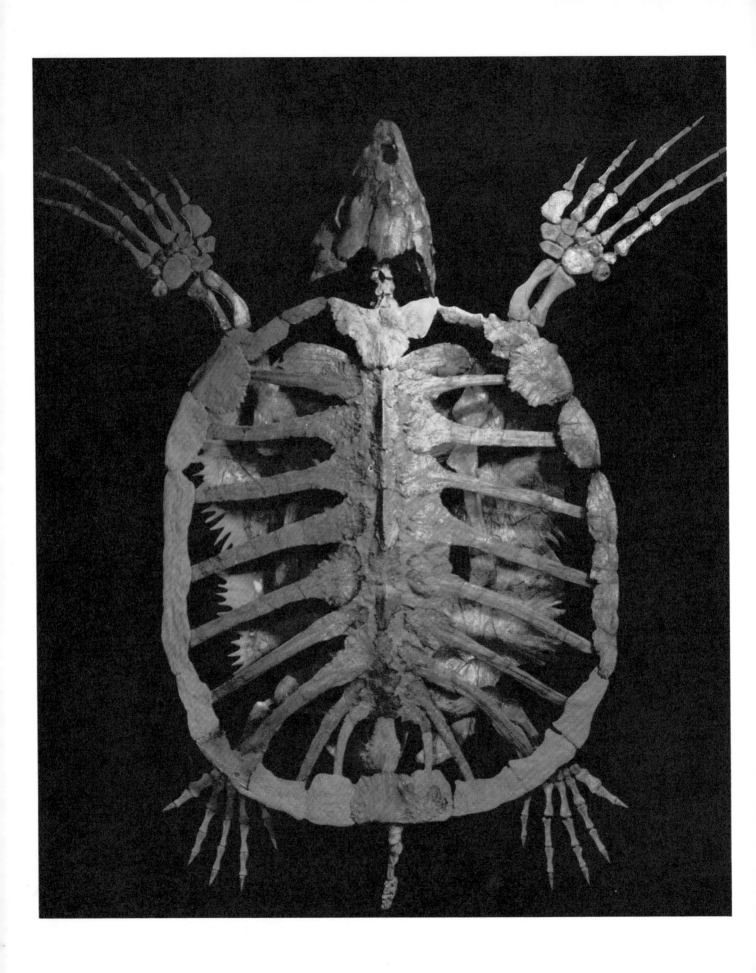

What are the ancestors of turtles?

This giant turtle was about 12 feet (3.5 m) long. Millions of years ago, it swam in the seas that covered the center of North America.

No one knows what the first ancestors of turtles were. The oldest known member of this group is *proganochelys,* which lived more than 200 million years ago. Even then, it looked very much like its present-day relative. This animal lived in what is now Germany. It grew about 3 feet (1 m) long and was covered by a solid shell. It also had a series of defensive spikes on its neck, feet, and tail. But it was not able to draw in, or retract, its body parts. A modern turtle can retract its body into its shell. Proganochelys also had a beak and teeth.

What did the first crocodiles look like?

The oldest crocodiles lived 200 million years ago. They were fairly small reptiles, barely growing more than 3 feet (1 m) long. They had short snouts and long limbs. These crocodiles were not as well adapted to the water as today's crocodiles are. Still, some of them did adapt fairly quickly to life in the water. Soon they were found in both the rivers and the seas. Seas covered much of the world at the time. One hundred and fifty million years ago, they lived there in large numbers.

Some crocodiles lived in fresh water. They became enormous. One type, *sarcosuchus,* grew to be nearly 33 feet long (10 m) long. It lived in Africa and South America.

For a long time, crocodiles roamed great areas of the land. They are no longer found in many of these areas today. This was due to the warmer climate of the time.

False and true crocodiles

Phytosaurs were also ancestors of the dinosaurs. They resembled crocodiles. A very similar way of living led both groups to take on the same appearance. But they were actually very different. Phytosaurs had nostrils placed near their eyes. A crocodile's nostrils, however, are at the end of its snout. Except for this, the two are easily confused.

A paleontologist removes the skull and jawbone of sarcosuchus from the sands of the Sahara. Sarcosuchus was the largest crocodile ever discovered. This animal lived 100 million years ago in Africa and South America. It was about 33 feet (10 m) long.

Why did some reptiles return to life in the water?

Hardly had the vertebrates adapted to the land when some of them returned to live in the oceans. To do this, they had to change again. Some of them changed very little. For example, the sea turtle's feet spread into swimming paddles. But its general shape remained like that of the land turtles. Reptiles of the Triassic period were amphibians rather than sea animals. They frequently returned to land and never ventured very far out to sea.

On the other hand, there was the group known as ichthyosaurs. These reptiles looked and acted very much like the present-day dolphins. They were very specialized creatures, as they were totally free from solid ground. The number of their fingers increased to form large flippers. Their necks shortened. Their tails resembled a shark's tail.

Births at sea

The ichthyosaurs never returned to land, even to lay eggs. They gave birth in the open sea. Some fossilized ichthyosaurs have shown that the mothers kept their eggs in their stomachs.

From well-preserved fossils, paleontologists can make accurate reconstructions. This specimen of an ichthyosaurus still has the imprint of its fins. This fossil was discovered in Germany.

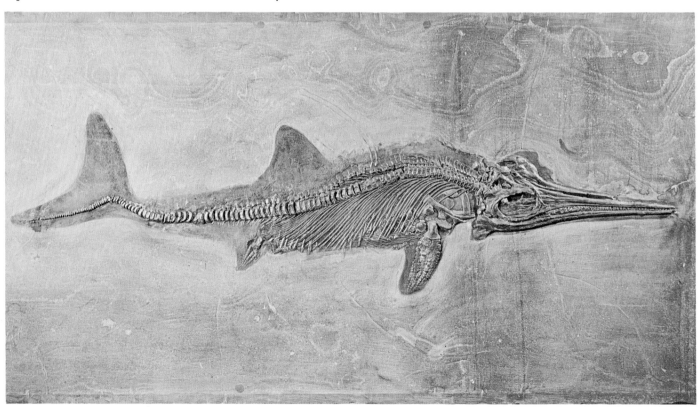

What were the largest sea reptiles?

Some kinds of ichthyosaurs grew to enormous sizes. One type, the *shonisaurus,* was discovered in Nevada (United States). This animal was 45 feet (14 m) long. However, most of them were not more than a few yards long.

During the Mesozoic era, the ichthyosaurs slowly gave up their place. Developing groups, such as the *plesiosaurs,* became rulers of the sea. The plesiosaurs were divided into two groups. Some of them had tiny heads and long necks. They also had stocky bodies and moved with four long flippers. During their evolution, their necks grew even longer. Eventually, some plesiosaurs had necks about 21 feet (6.5 m) long. The other group had much smaller necks. But these necks supported enormous heads with terrible teeth. The biggest of them was *kronosaurus* of Australia. This monster was 36 feet (11 m) long.

The skeleton of a pliosaurus lies under a protective roof. The pliosaurus was a sea monster of the Mesozoic era. The pliosaurus had a long, oval body with large paddles. Its head was narrow and had a long snout with rows of sharp teeth.

The plesiosaurs—and large reptiles in general—have always excited the imagination. Here a plesiosaurus is featured on the cover of a French magazine.

What did sea reptiles eat?

Even the teeth of an animal can tell a lot about it. Teeth of sea reptiles from the Mesozoic era show that the reptiles were carnivores. Toward the end of this era, the bony fish of the modern type were multiplying. They provided an easy food source for these sea vertebrates. These vertebrates also fed on mollusks and animals close to modern squid and cuttlefish. One of these animals was the belemnite. This creature was a lot like the cuttlefish. Many belemnites have been found in the stomachs of certain ichthy-osaurs. Another tempting prey was the ammonite. This creature is recognized by its curled shell. Paleontologists even spotted teethmarks from a sea vertebrate on a large ammonite found in South Dakota (United States).

Hunting methods varied according to the prey and the hunters. The ichthyosaurs used their speed to hunt. The *mosasaurs* used their flexibility. The less agile plesiosaurs made use of their long necks. With them, they plunged their heads into schools of fish. Finally, the *kronosaurs* were super predators of the sea. Animals in this group attacked other large vertebrates. This is similar to the way that today's killer whales attack sperm whales.

Sea animals known as ammonites were abundant in the Mesozoic era. They became an easy food source for the bigger sea reptiles.

The "flying dragon" from the Sunda Islands is an example of a flying lizard. The first flying lizards of the Paleozoic era probably looked like this.

What were the first flying vertebrates?

At the start of the Mesozoic era, or even earlier, small vertebrates had become well adapted to life in the trees. They then tried to make use of the air. Using flight, they escaped their enemies. Later, they even learned to hunt for insects this way.

Lizards like the present-day "flying dragon" were able to fly using a large body membrane. This membrane stretched from one side of a lizard's body to the other on long movable sticks. These sticks were in fact modified ribs.

Podopteryx was a thecodont from the Triassic period. It was found in Central Asia. The podopteryx had a large piece of skin attached to its limbs and tail. It was a little like a flying squirrel. This animal knew how to glide after launching itself into the air.

THE REIGN
OF THE DINOSAURS

What is the origin of the dinosaurs?

The word *dinosaur* comes from two Greek words meaning "terrible lizard." Dinosaurs include two groups of reptiles, both of which are extinct today. They made their appearance during the Triassic period, the first period of the Mesozoic era. That was about 215 million years ago. Dinosaurs descended from an order of animals known as thecodonts. Thecodonts were active, meat-eating animals that traveled on foot rather than crawling. From this one large group two groups of dinosaurs emerged.

It is important to remember that dinosaurs lived only on land. Other prehistoric animals lived alongside the dinosaurs. These included the two large groups of sea reptiles: the ichthyosaurs and the plesiosaurs. Flying reptiles of the *pterosaurs* order also existed during this time. But because none of these reptiles lived on land, they were not considered dinosaurs.

The oldest dinosaurs were fairly small and agile animals. Some ate meat, and others ate plants. Soon, some dinosaurs grew very large. The longest were about 90 feet (27 m) long.

In southern England in 1822, Gideon and Mary Mantell made one of the first dinosaur discoveries. Mary Mantell first found several teeth of a fossilized animal. Gideon Mantell later found the animal's bones. The Mantells named this animal *iguanodon*. An English paleontologist, Sir Richard Owen, grouped such animals under the name *dinosaurs*. This means "terrible lizards." This 1853 etching pokes fun at Owen and other paleontologists. Here, they hold a banquet to celebrate their science. A reconstructed iguanodon serves as their banquet hall.

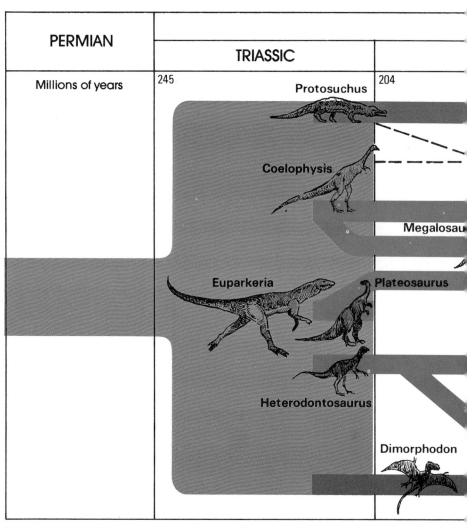

PERMIAN	TRIASSIC	
Millions of years	245	204

Protosuchus

Coelophysis

Megalosau

Euparkeria

Plateosaurus

Heterodontosaurus

Dimorphodon

The evolution of dinosaurs and their close relatives.

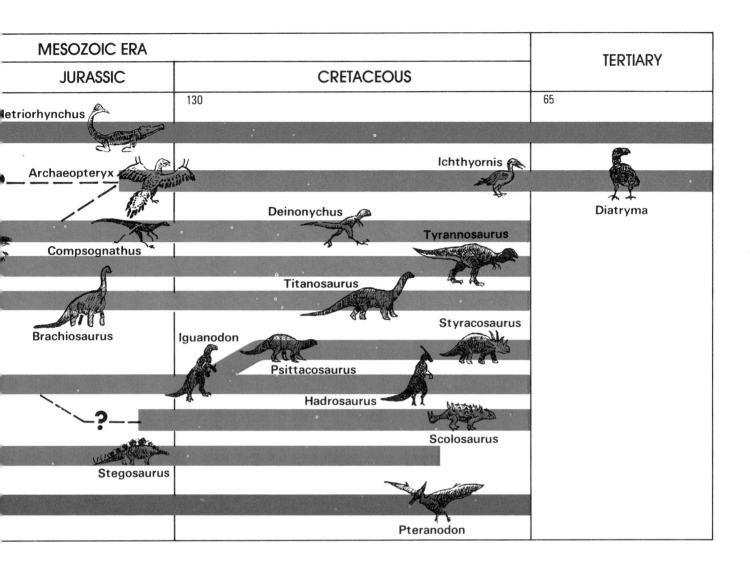

| MESOZOIC ERA | | TERTIARY |
| JURASSIC | CRETACEOUS | |

What are the main groups of dinosaurs?

The two main dinosaur groups, or orders, are identified by their pelvic bones. Dinosaurs had three bones in the hip. In each group, these were arranged differently. The first group is called the *saurischians,* which means "lizard hipped." These dinosaurs had lizard-like hip structures. The other group is the *ornithischians.* This name means "bird pelvis." These dinosaurs had bird-like hip structures. Each of these two large groups had several very different forms.

The main kinds of saurischians were the *sauropods* and the *theropods.* The sauropods were giants of the dinosaur world. Many were about 70 feet (21 m) long. They walked on four heavy legs and had tiny heads. Their necks and tails, however, were very long. The theropods were fearsome, two-legged dinosaurs. They had strong jaws with many cutting teeth. They were the only meat-eating dinosaurs.

There were four main types of ornithischians: *ornithopods, stegosaurs, ankylosaurs,* and *ceratopsians.* All of them ate plants. The ornithopods had jaws that ended in beak-like structures. Some were two-legged animals. The four-legged stegosaurs had rows of bony plates on their backs. The ankylosaurs were known as the armored dinosaurs. Finally there were the four-legged ceratopsians. These dinosaurs had huge heads with horns.

37

Where have dinosaurs been found?

The first dinosaurs were discovered in England in 1822. Since then, dinosaur remains have been found in many areas of the world. These places include: the Rocky Mountains, the jungles of Thailand, the polar regions, and even the Sahara Desert. Two American paleontologists, Othniel Charles Marsh and Edward Drinker Cope, made the American West particularly famous for research. Each of them wanted to discover the most new dinosaurs. Their crews actually came to blows over this. Very important beds were also discovered in Canada, Africa, Mongolia, and Nigeria. Dinosaur remains have also been found in South America and Australia.

Many well-preserved dinosaurs have been found in Europe. A beautiful discovery was made in Bernissart, Belgium, in 1878. Some miners discovered about thirty *iguanodon* skeletons in a coal mine. But finds are not always this spectacular. Often, nothing but a few isolated bones are found. But all of the discoveries together show that dinosaurs lived on all continents. At that time, the world was not as it is today. The areas where dinosaurs roamed were very different in terms of climate, landscape, and plant life. Today, research continues, and every year paleontologists gather new dinosaur bones.

The dinosaurs of France

Southern France is especially rich in dinosaur bones and eggs from the Mesozoic era. Sauropods, theropods, ornithopods, and ankylosaurs all lived there at that time. The most complete dinosaur skeleton discovered in France is hardly larger than a cat's skeleton. This is the skeleton of compsognathus. It is 140 million years old. It was discovered in a quarry.

Were all dinosaurs big?

● CRETACEOUS

■ JURASSIC

▲ TRIASSIC

As this map shows, dinosaurs have been discovered throughout the entire world. Every year, new beds are discovered. Beds, or sites, are places where remains have been found.

Dinosaurs are generally thought of as giants. Many of them did grow to enormous sizes. Those belonging to the sauropods group were the giants. Some large sauropods, like the *diplodocus,* were nearly 90 feet (27 m) long. The largest of all was the *brachiosaurus.* It weighed up to eighty-five tons. But not all dinosaurs were this huge. Some were much smaller. Some, like the *compsognathus,* were no bigger than a cat. This small dinosaur belonged to the the theropods group. It lived some 140 million years ago in Bavaria and France.

Which were the strangest dinosaurs?

The ankylosaurus and the stegosaurus were two very strange dinosaurs. The ankylosaurus was built like a military tank. An armor-like shell, covered with spikes, protected its body. The stegosaurus was protected by upright plates that ran from its neck to its tail.

It is very hard to determine the most unusual dinosaurs. Many of them looked odd. Among the sauropods, the enormous brachiosaurus was strange looking. This animal had front feet that were longer than its back feet. It carried its head 36 feet (11 m) off the ground. The theropod *deinonychus* lived about 110 million years ago in North America. This animal was interesting because of the huge sickle-shaped claw on the second toe of each of its hind legs. The deinonychus must have used this claw to open the belly of its prey.

The ornithischians were no less surprising. The "duckbilled dinosaurs" or *hadrosaurs*, which lived toward the end of the Mesozoic era, are good examples of this. Their jaws, equipped with many teeth, ended in a flat bill, like a duck's. Many of them had strange, crest-shaped heads. The nasal passages extended into these. Perhaps they used these to amplify their cries.

The *stegoceras* lived at the same time as the duckbilled dinosaur. It was just as odd. In spite of its bulging head, it had a very small brain. The bones of its skull were very

thick and may have been used for fighting. Scientists think the males fought by butting heads, like rams do today.

Members of the stegosaurs group all had very strange appearances. They all had armors with rows of large plates or bony points running down their backs. Perhaps these plates were used to control body temperature.

The ankylosaurs have been called "reptile tanks" because of their well-developed armor. Some of them even had spiked clubs at the ends of their tails.

Then there were the ceratopsians. These were better known as the horned dinosaurs. The *pachyrhinosaurus* was one of the most interesting. It did not have a horn. Instead, it had a bony plate between its eyes. Another ceratopsian, the *styracosaurus* had many horns on a collar that covered the back of its head.

What did dinosaurs eat?

Paleontologists can guess what dinosaurs ate by studying the shape of their jaws and teeth. The large theropods had powerful jaws and huge, notched teeth. With these teeth, these dinosaurs tore the flesh of their prey. These animals must have been fierce carnivores which fed on other large reptiles.

The other dinosaurs were all herbivores, or plant-eaters. This is shown by their teeth, which were used to cut and mash plants. But they did not all eat the same plants. The large sauropods had weak jaws and small teeth. They probably ate tender water plants. But their long necks may have been used to reach leaves in the treetops, too. The stegosaurs and ankylosaurs had very small teeth. Scientists are not sure what they ate. On the other hand, the duckbilled dinosaurs had many teeth. These were arranged so that the worn teeth were constantly replaced by others. This allowed them to crush even the toughest plants. Lastly, the ceratopsians had many teeth. They could eat fairly hard plants.

The terrible jaws of the tyrannosaurus leave no doubt about its diet. This carnivore was even able to attack large plant-eating dinosaurs.

Have dinosaur eggs ever been discovered?

In 1922, an American expedition discovered the remains of fossilized eggs in the Gobi Desert. These were first thought to be large bird eggs. The next year, more eggs were found in the same bed. These eggs were intact. From them, it was possible to determine that they had been laid by dinosaurs. Many dinosaur bones were found nearby.

The bones belonged to a dinosaur called *protoceratops*. This animal grew to be 6 feet (2 m) long. It had a collar covering the back of its head, but no horns. Its eggs, which were very long, had a rough surface. Some were still arranged in a circle in nests dug in the sand. One nest contained eighteen eggs. Perhaps the bones belonged to a female protoceratops, and she died guarding her eggs. A Polish expedition found the interwoven skeletons of a protoceratops and a small two-legged dinosaur. These were probably the result of mortal combat with an egg thief.

Dinosaur eggs have also been found in other areas. The most spectacular beds are those in southern France. Many eggs have been found there. These eggs are nearly round and much larger than those of the protoceratops.

Many dinosaur eggs have been discovered in southern France. This one is about 8 inches (20 cm) long. Shells in such perfect condition are rare. But fragments are common.

How did dinosaurs walk?

To imagine how a dinosaur walked, paleontologists use its skeleton as a guide. From studies, they can see that the large sauropods must have walked on four powerful limbs. The same is true for the stegosaurs, ankylosaurs, and ceratopsians. These massive animals could not have stood upright.

On the other hand, some dinosaurs had very small front legs. Theropods such as the *tyrannosaurus* obviously walked only on their hind legs. They used their strong tails for balance or support. Ornithopods probably had animals of both kinds. Some probably stood on two legs; others stood on four.

In addition to skeletons, paleontologists also study dinosaur footprints. In many parts of the world, footprints have been found on the surfaces of rocks. These were probably left there while the rock was still mud. From this, it is possible to learn how various dinosaurs traveled and even how fast they moved.

The ceratopsians used a different means of defense. These dinosaurs had long pointed horns. Against these, even the tyrannosaurus was not safe. It is harder to guess how the sauropods defended themselves. They had no armor or horns. Perhaps they hid in the water. Many carnivores would not follow them there.

How did herbivorous dinosaurs defend themselves?

The triceratops was very capable of defending itself. It was heavily built with strong legs and had long, sharp horns.

Herbivorous, or plant-eating, dinosaurs must have often faced attacks from large carnivores. But they had ways of defending themselves against these masses of teeth and claws. For the lightest, quickest herbivores, like certain small ornithopods, running was the simplest solution. The very large carnivores could not have been as fast. But the bigger herbivores could not do this. They were forced to confront their enemies. Luckily, they had various "weapons" to defend themselves.

The stegosaurs and ankylosaurs used protective armor. This armor was made of bony plates covering the animal's back, sides, or even the entire body. The tail often had a group of long spines or a sort of bony mass. It was used for striking fatal blows against an enemy.

What animals ruled the air during the time of the dinosaurs?

During the Mesozoic era, reptiles ruled not only the land and sea, but also the air. Those which adapted best to it were the pterosaurs. These reptiles were distant relatives of the dinosaurs and crocodiles. Their wings were actually membranes attached to the bones of their arms. Their skeletons were very light because their bones were hollow and had very thin walls. It is thought that one of the largest pterosaurs, *pteranodon,* weighed barely 26 pounds (12 kg). And this was an animal with a 21-foot (6 m) wingspan. With the slightest gust of wind, this animal could take flight. Then, using air currents, it could stay in the air a very long time.

The first pterosaurs had long tails. These may have been used as rudders. They also had sharp teeth with which they could seize small prey. Eventually, their tails and teeth became smaller. Some of them, like pteranodon, had nothing more than a solid beak without teeth. The size of these reptiles varied greatly. The *pterodactylus* was hardly bigger than a crow. Other later forms were larger than the pteranodon.

The pterosaurs were the ancestors of neither birds nor bats. Their wings had totally different designs. They became extinct at the end of the Mesozoic era, with no descendants. This left the birds as masters of the air.

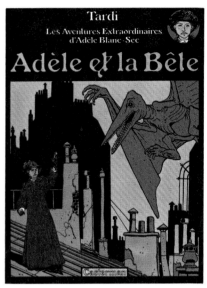

When comic strips and paleontology meet. . . .

The fur of flying reptiles

The pterosaurs were quite strange reptiles. They are thought to have been covered with fur. Traces of fur were found over fifty years ago on fossils in Germany. In 1971, an excellent specimen was discovered in Russia. Its imprint showed that a thick fur covered the bodies of these animals. Undoubtedly it helped them conserve body temperature.

Not all flying reptiles were gigantic. This pterodactylus was hardly any larger than a crow. Its skeleton was found in Bavaria. The bed from which it came also contained the oldest known bird.

Which was the largest flying animal of all?

For a long time, pteranodon, with its 21 foot (6 m) wingspan, was considered the largest flying reptile. But recently, in Texas, the remains of an even more gigantic member of this group has been found. Called *quetzalcoatlus,* its wingspan must have reached about 36 feet (11 m). This giant lived at the end of the Mesozoic era. It seems to have been the largest flying animal that ever existed. Its way of life is not very well known.

Did birds exist during the time of the dinosaurs?

One hundred forty million years ago, when the dinosaurs reigned, birds already existed. The oldest known is archaeopteryx. Five skeletons of this animal have been found in very fine limestone in Bavaria. The fineness of these rocks made it possible to preserve its feather prints. If they had not been preserved, no one would have known that it was a bird, because archaeopteryx looked much more like a reptile. Nearly the size of a pigeon, it had a long tail. It also had claws on its wings and teeth in its jaws. Studies of its skeleton make experts think that archaeopteryx did not fly very well. Its feathers, however, were similar to the feathers of birds today.

Only five skeletons of archaeopteryx have been discovered in over a century. All of them were found in Bavaria. With the skeletons, paleontologists have made exact replicas of the animal.

The discovery of the first archaeopteryx

The first skeleton of archaeopteryx was found in a limestone quarry in Bavaria in 1861. It was acquired by a doctor, who sold it to the highest bidder. The British Museum in London bought it for 700 pounds sterling. This was a very high price at the time. Any skeletons discovered since that time have remained in Germany.

Why did the dinosaurs disappear?

At the end of the Mesozoic era, 65 million years ago, all dinosaurs became extinct. These animals had ruled the earth for 150 million years. Their disappearance made way for the smaller reptiles and mammals. The end of the large reptiles remains one of the most mysterious events in the history of living creatures. Paleontologists have many theories to explain it.

Some think that mammals became a threat to the dinosaurs. For example, mammals may have eaten their eggs. But, dinosaurs and mammals had lived together for 150 million years before the dinosaurs disappeared. So, this idea does not seem very likely.

Recently, scientists have done studies on rocks from the dinosaur age. In them, they found strange chemical compounds. These compounds have led them to believe that an enormous meteorite struck the earth during that time. This disaster would have caused the dinosaurs to die out. But other animals, such as crocodiles, turtles, birds, and mammals survived. How can this be explained?

It is also possible that the climate changed at the end of the Mesozoic era. It is known that the level of the seas greatly decreased at this time. This would certainly have caused strange climate changes. Perhaps this caused the temperature to drop and the seasons to become more distinct. Temperatures had been high during the dinosaurs' reign. Without becoming very cold, the climate could have changed enough to change plant life. The dinosaurs could not have adapted to this new environment quickly enough.

To stay in the air, birds must flap their wings continuously. It takes a lot of strength. The ancient bird, archaeopteryx, was able to fly. But its wing muscles were not nearly as developed. Therefore, it was not nearly as skillful in the air as today's birds are.

Did other animals disappear at the same time as the dinosaurs?

At the end of their history, certain ammonites took on strange shapes. They disappeared at about the same time as the dinosaurs.

Dinosaurs disappeared at the end of the Mesozoic era. But during this time, many other animals also disappeared. In the air, the pterosaurs made way for the birds. However, in the seas, the reptiles became extinct too. But the vertebrates were not the only ones to suffer. The sea mollusks had been very numerous during the Mesozoic era. But they did not last beyond the lower limits of the Tertiary period. The ammonites, belemnites, and rudistoids also died out. Their column-shaped shells formed huge reefs.

To explain all these disappearances, experts need to find the common point that unites these creatures. They all lived in very different environments. So their living conditions would all have been very different. In fact, groups occupying some of these same environments survived without any difficulty. This problem remains unsolved today.

What reptiles outlived the dinosaurs?

At the start of the Tertiary period, dinosaurs no longer existed. But this does not mean that all the reptiles disappeared. Turtles and crocodiles still played an important role. Lizards and snakes made up another important group. Their evolution has continued up to the present day. Large sea lizards, however, disappeared at the end of the Cretaceous period. Although they and other large reptiles were not seen again, their relatives never stopped spreading.

Not all reptiles became extinct with the dinosaurs. Sea turtles have survived for tens of millions of years.

THE RISE OF MAMMALS

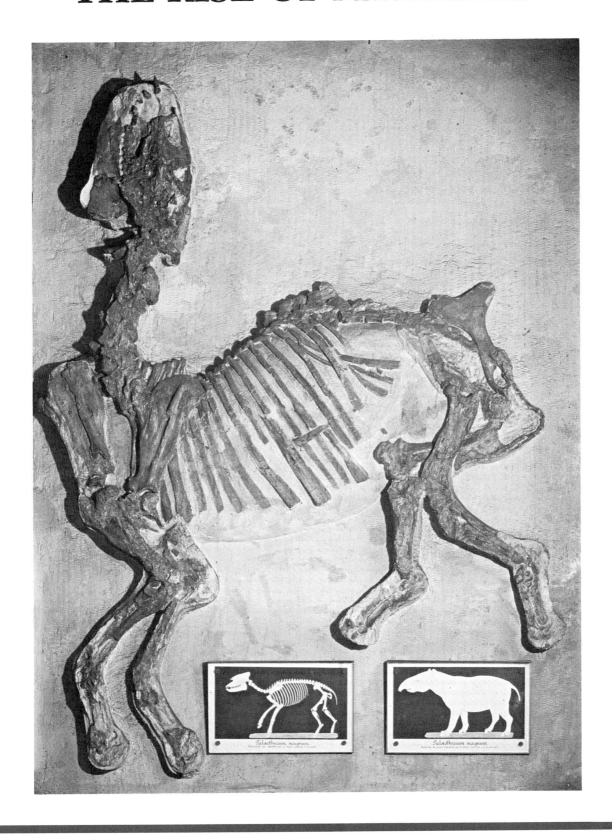

What animals replaced the large reptiles on land?

Diatryma was a huge carnivorous bird. Fossils of it have been found in North America and Europe.

The term *reptile* can refer to a stage of evolution. Many groups of vertebrates have passed through this stage. Those that did not evolve any further are called reptiles. Turtles, snakes, lizards, crocodiles, pterosaurs, dinosaurs, and ichthyosaurs are all reptiles. However, two groups went through a reptilian stage and continued to evolve. This was the case with birds and mammals. At the start of the Tertiary era, they began to fill the holes left by the vanishing dinosaurs.

Gigantic birds were the first replacements for the predator dinosaurs. Their bones have been discovered in Europe and America. With their useless wings, they could no longer fly. But, to make up for it, they developed strong legs and feet. These allowed the giant birds to run fast enough to catch the large mammals. One, called *diatryma,* was 6 feet (2 m) high. It had an enormous parrot's beak. Its body was covered with fibrous feathers. Many fossilized examples of these have been found.

Mammals had been rare during the Mesozoic era. They now multiplied rapidly. However, the groups that became most important in the new era, called Cenozoic, already existed. Primates, for example, were already defined. But it was not until the Cenozoic era that the mammals really began to dominate. Mammals have since been called the most adaptable group of animals ever known.

Are horses very ancient animals?

The horse can be traced from the very small hyracotherium to the modern-day horse. This is an excellent example of evolution.

The oldest known ancestor of the horse is a small hoofed animal, called *hyracotherium.* It lived in North America and Europe at the start of the Tertiary period. Hyracotherium was no larger than a small dog. It had four toes on its front hooves and three toes on its back hooves. The structure of its teeth show that it ate tender leaves. Its descendants were larger. They broke into several different groups. The most important of these groups led to the horse. Its development took place almost completely in North America.

Toward the end of the Tertiary period, the climate was drier. The forests gave way to vast prairies covered with grass. The food on these prairies was tougher to digest. Horses developed teeth that could act as powerful grindstones. At the same time, horses began to increase in size. The number of toes decreased.

These animals continued to change. Their legs grew increasingly longer. With them, the animals were able to run ever faster. In the Quaternary period, these animals gave birth to *equus,* the present-day horse.

What relatives of the horse are extinct?

Horses belong to an order known as *perissodactyla*. Today this group includes only a few species of animals (horses and their close relatives, rhinoceroses, and tapirs). All animals in this group share one important characteristic. That is, they are odd-toed. Each foot has a hoof containing one or three toes. This sets these animals apart from the cow, the sheep, and the pig, which have an even number of toes.

This order used to include many other species of animals. Some of these were relatives of the horse. Many are now extinct. These include the *brontotheres* which lived in North America and Asia. They were originally small in size and looked like hyracotherium. But after a rapid evolution, these animals grew as large as rhinoceroses. They also developed powerful, bony forks on their noses. The purpose of these is still unclear.

The *chalicotheres* were even stranger. They had horse-like heads and bodies supported by large clawed feet. This combination seemed impossible to many paleontologists. For a long time, its remains were thought to be from two different animals.

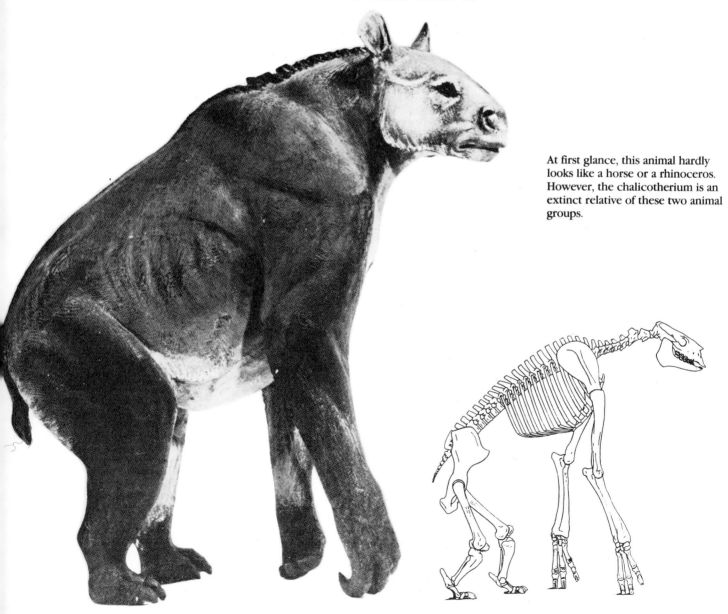

At first glance, this animal hardly looks like a horse or a rhinoceros. However, the chalicotherium is an extinct relative of these two animal groups.

The teeth and skeleton of indricotherium have given paleontologists much information about the animal. Because of these remains, experts now classify it among the rhinoceroses. However, its looks alone would not have led to this conclusion.

Skull of arsinoitherium

Did the rhinoceros always have horns?

The rhino's horn is probably its most noticeable trait. But about 40 million years ago, the first rhinoceroses did not have horns. These slender animals looked something like small horses. Some of their descendants began to grow larger, but they still did not have horns. Some early rhinoceroses were short-legged. They walked a little bit like the hippopotamus and lived in the water part of the time. Others grew to giant sizes. The largest known land mammal was *indricotherium*. This was an enormous, hornless rhinoceros. It grew more than 15 feet (4.5 m) high and lived in Asia.

When horned rhinoceroses appeared, they spread all over the world. Today, they are found only in Africa and southern Asia. But they also once lived in North America and Europe. Prehistoric people hunted the last European rhinoceroses.

Arsinoitherium: a false rhinoceros.

The first rhinoceroses did not have any horns. Other animals existing at the same time had well developed ones. This was the case with the arsinoitherium. This animal had a pair of huge horns on its nose. However it was not related to the rhinoceros.

These two animals (deinotherium above, amebelodon below) are related to the modern-day elephant.

What were the ancestors of the elephants?

The remains of an animal named *moeritherium* were found in Egypt. They were found in rocks dating from about 40 million years ago. This animal is a primitive relative of the elephant. It only slightly resembles the modern-day elephant. It grew as a tapir, but had short legs and no trunk. It probably spent part of its time in the water.

Somewhat later, animals like *paleomastodon* appeared. This animal was larger than moeritherium. It had longer limbs and a short trunk. These primitive mastodons had a pair of tusks on each jaw, a total of four tusks. Their short molars were covered with many bumps.

About 25 million years ago, mastodons spread from Africa into many areas of the world. The true elephants descended from some of them. They appeared at the end of the Tertiary period. These animals had only one pair of tusks on their upper jaws. Their strong molars pointed upward, allowing them to chew tough plants.

During the Tertiary period, an animal called *deinotherium* lived in Africa, Asia, and Europe. The deinotherium was a strange relative of the mastodons and elephants. It had tusks only on its lower jaw and they curved downward.

What animals populated the first great prairies?

During the Tertiary period, the first great prairies and savannas appeared. Before this, herbivores had lived mainly in the forests. Now, to survive in these vast expanses of grass, they were forced to change. They adapted to the new diet by developing longer, stronger teeth. Eating grass wears teeth down faster than eating leaves does. Also, in the open plains, herbivores were less able to hide from carnivorous enemies. Animals that could not defend themselves needed to have long legs. With long legs they were able to run away fast. Some animals were able to chew cud. This means they could swallow the plant food and chew it later. This meant that they spent less time feeding.

Fifteen million years ago, savannas covered southern Europe. They were inhabited by large herds of *hipparion,* a primitive three-toed horse. This horse lived alongside antelopes and giraffes (whose necks were still short). Rhinoceroses, mastodons, and the strange *chalicotheres* were found there, too.

At about the same time, North America was also populated by rhinoceroses, mastodons, and three-toed horses. But camels could also be found there. Some of them had very long legs and long necks. They looked like giraffes. Many strange herbivores also lived in the North American prairies. These looked somewhat like antelopes, but they had strange horns on their snouts.

Did the first giraffes have long necks?

The first giraffes were small and slender. They probably looked more like deer than the majestic beasts living on the African savannas. But over time, their size increased. Fifteen million years ago, animals like the okapi were already living in southern Europe. The okapi is related to the giraffe and lives in the forests of the Congo. These primitive giraffes did not yet have long necks. But some of them had impressive horns. One, called the *sivatherium,* lived in Asia and Africa during the Tertiary period. It had strange twisted antlers.

The modern-day okapi was not discovered until the start of this century. Fossilized giraffes resembling it were already known at that time.

When did the carnivorous mammals appear?

At the beginning of the Tertiary period, many mammals were omnivorous. This means they ate both plants and animals. Over time, some stopped eating anything except plants. But others attacked and ate herbivores. The first meat-eaters were not large. Their size increased as the prey became larger.

At the start of the Tertiary period, the ancestors of modern-day carnivores were still small. They were probably comparable to ferrets. They had long bodies and short legs. This early group of meat-eating mammals were called *creodons*. Some of them looked like dogs. Others looked like hyenas. Still others looked like cats, and they sometimes grew to large sizes. But in the end they became extinct when faced with competition from the true carnivores.

About the middle of the Tertiary period, true carnivores separated into two large groups. One group was known as the *canoidae*. This group was very dog-like. It now includes wolves, bears, raccoons, and weasels. Early members of this group were similar to the wolves or wild dogs of today. Others looked much stranger. About 20 million years ago there existed a kind of "hyena-dog" and "bear-dog." The first true bears were quite small, but their size increased rapidly. The other group developed into very cat-like animals. This group is known as the *feloidae* and includes genets, hyenas, and cats.

How did saber-toothed cats kill their prey?

Several times in the evolution of cats, there appeared large felines. Some, like *machairodus* and *smilodon,* had long, flat, upper canine teeth. These teeth looked like the blades of a saber. This earned these animals the nickname "saber-toothed tigers." When their mouths were closed, these teeth stuck out from each side of the lower jaw. These fierce animals must have often terrorized the large herbivores.

These saber-like teeth were most likely used to stab prey. These felines were able to open their mouths very wide. This and their powerful neck muscles allowed them to strike their victims brutally. Stabbing with their teeth, the big felines mortally wounded their prey. But these terrible predators must have had a hard time chewing meat. Perhaps they ate only the animal's blood and intestines. Remains from the feline, smilodon, have been found in many places, including the famous La Brea tar pits of California. This animal was the last and the largest of the saber-toothed cats.

Prehistoric people knew the terrible saber-toothed tigers. In America, smilodon became extinct more recently than its European cousins.

Why are the animals of Australia so strange?

The first European explorers of Australia were stunned by the strange plant and animal life that they found there. Everything there seemed so different than in Europe. The swans were black. Duckbilled mammals laid eggs. The continent was dominated by marsupials. Marsupials are mammals whose babies stay in their mother's belly only a short time. They finish their development in her external pouch. On the other hand, placentals are rare there. Placental mammals' young develop in the mother's body. The babies of these animals are born completely formed.

The separation of the two groups dates back to the Mesozoic era. Australia, however, has been totally isolated since that time. Because of this, the development of other wildlife forms was rare. Without competition, marsupials developed a wide variety of forms.

However, some of the marsupials copied placental models. This is understandable in that these species have the same roles in nature. For example, there are "marsupial moles" and "marsupial cats." These animals have no relationship to the placental animals of the same name. They do, however, look very much alike. The only placentals that did reach Australia were bats and rodents. Later, many species came as people did. These included animals such as dogs and rabbits.

Several million years ago, the Australian wildlife included large marsupials. The diptrodon, shown here, was as big as a rhinoceros.

The koala is one of the most famous marsupials. It feeds only on eucalyptus leaves. This specialized diet makes it hard for the koala to survive outside of its natural environment.

Were other continents as isolated as Australia?

Marsupials reigned supreme in Australia. But this does not mean they were absent from other areas. In South America they lived alongside the placentals. These two continents are very far apart today. But some experts think that they were connected in the past.

In fact, some people think that Australia, Antarctica, and South America were all once a single mass. According to this idea, the mass broke apart during the Cretaceous period. This was caused by the shifting motion of the land masses known as continental drift. Before, this land mass belonged to the marsupials. Whereas in Europe, Asia, Africa, and North America the mammals took placental forms. Some of them, however, went from North America to South America before South America was isolated.

During the Tertiary period, unique life forms developed there. These consisted of a mix of marsup-

Sloths living today make their homes in trees. But the gigantic sloth, megatherium, was exclusively a land animal. Its remains were discovered in South America a long time ago.

ials and placentals that were unknown anywhere else. Strangely, these marsupials fed on animal prey like the land birds and stange land crocodiles. The placentals, however, remained herbivores. The only outsiders were rodents and apes. They came from Africa in the middle of the Tertiary period. At the end of this period, communications were reestablished between the two parts of America. The animals of North America then invaded the South.

Where and when did the giant birds live?

At the start of the Tertiary period, large land birds were fierce predators. But carnivorous placentals developed rapidly. This soon caused the extinction of these birds. This was not the case, however, in South America where marsupials lived. There, the giant birds thrived until the end of the Tertiary era. They grew to monstrous sizes. The *phororhacos* was a bird that hunted herbi-

vores in Patagonia. Its skull alone was 24 inches (61 cm) long.

Certain peaceful birds lived on isolated islands until recent times. Safe from carnivores, birds populated islands such as New Zealand. There, people known as the Maoris saw the last of the *dinornis.* This bird stood 10 feet (3 m) tall. And in Madagascar, the huge eggs of the extinct *aepyornis* are still found.

Mammoths became extinct a few thousand years ago. People may have exterminated them. The remains of the mammoth are often found in the frozen soil of Siberia. Their tusks have been an important source of ivory for a long time. Chinese craftsmen often used them.

How did the mammals adapt to glacial periods?

At the end of the Tertiary period, the climate cooled. The earth experienced glacial periods. At that time, the polar cap reached as far as northern Germany. The mountain ranges were covered by gigantic glaciers. Animals like the hippopotamus, which still played in the Seine River (France) in the Quaternary period, moved to warmer areas. Others became extinct. Animals better suited to the cold settled in.

Reindeer and musk oxen grazed in southern France. Others, such as the wooly mammoths and rhinoceroses, were also found there. These animals, which are the most gigantic of land animals, are extinct today. They were protected from the cold by their fleece. With it, these animals were like radiators, heating and holding the air that they breathed.

GEOLOGICAL TIME SCALE

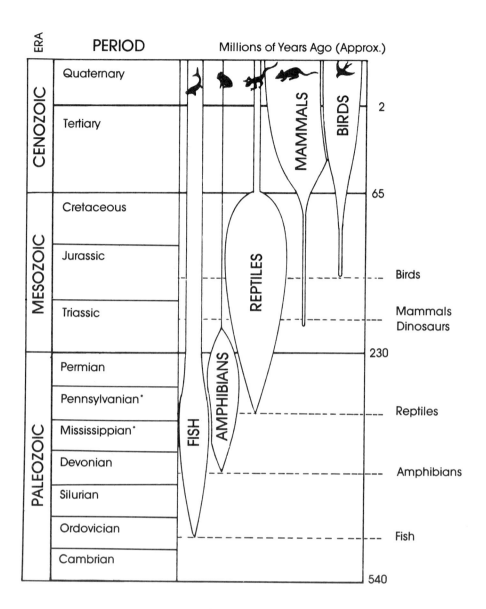

*The Pennsylvanian and Mississippian periods are often
linked together in the Carboniferous period.

Glossary

algae a group of mainly aquatic (water) plants without true stems, roots, or leaves, but containing chlorophyll. Seaweed is one type of alga.

amber a dark yellow stone-like material formed from fossilized resin. Amber is found chiefly along the Baltic Sea coasts in Germany and Russia. It is used for making decorative objects, especially jewelry.

amphibian a cold-blooded, smooth-skinned animal with a backbone that lives both on land and in the water.

anatomy the structure of a plant or animal.

carnivore an animal that feeds mainly on the flesh of other animals.

cartilage a strong body material, softer than bone, like the inside of the human nose.

Cenozoic era the most recent era in the geologic time scale of the earth's history. Sometimes called the Age of Mammals, it is marked by the rapid evolution of mammals, birds, and many plants.

cold-blooded having a body temperature that changes with the air or water of the surroundings.

continental drift a theory that says that the continents have moved great distances on the earth's surface and are still moving today. According to the theory, the continents once formed a single land mass called *Pangaea*.

convergence the development of similar characteristics often resulting from a similarity of habits or environments.

crustacean any of a large class of animals whose bodies are covered with hard, shell-like coverings. Lobsters, shrimp, and crabs are crustaceans.

Darwin (Charles) a British naturalist who became famous for his theories on evolution.

dinosaur any of a group of various extinct reptiles of the orders saurischia and ornithischia. Dinosaurs were only found on land and sometimes grew to giant sizes.

dorsal fin a fin found along an animal's back. On many aquatic animals, the dorsal fin is important for steering and balance.

embryo an organism in its early developmental stages, especially before birth.

epoch a division of geologic time that is less than a period and greater than an age.

era one of the five major divisions of geologic time. These five include the Cenozoic, Mesozoic, Paleozoic, Proterozoic, and Archeozoic eras.

evolution a gradual process of change or development. Many scientists believe that the theory of evolution explains the existence of today's plant and animal species. The theory says that existing plants and animals developed from previously existing species through this process of gradual change.

extinct no longer existing on the earth.

fossil remains of an animal or plant that lived millions of years ago.

herbivore an animal that feeds mainly on plants.

imprint a mark or depression made by pressure.

invertebrate lacking a backbone or spinal column.

lizard a four-legged animal with a long body, tapering tail, and scaly skin.

mammal a member of a group of warm-blooded animals. The mammal's characteristics include having a backbone and usually having hair or fur. All female mammals, including humans, secrete milk to feed their young.

marsupial any of an order of pouched mammals. In marsupials, the young begin development inside the mother's body, but finish their development in an external pouch. Marsupials are commonly found in Australia and South America. They include animals such as kangaroos, koala bears, wombats, etc.

Mesozoic era the geologic era of time between the Paleozoic and Cenozoic eras, sometimes called the Age of Reptiles. The Mesozoic era is marked by the presence of dinosaurs, marine and flying reptiles, etc.

omnivore an animal that feeds on both plant and animal matter.

ornithischia one of two main orders of dinosaurs. Ornithischians were known for bird-like hip structures.

paleontologist a scientist who studies fossils to find out about life during other periods of time.

Paleozoic era the era of geologic time before the Mesozoic era which began about 600 million years ago. Invertebrates were dominant during this time. Amphibians and reptiles began to appear in the later periods of this era.

period a division of geologic time longer than an epoch and included in an era.

placental any of an order of mammals whose young are fully developed in the mother's body before birth.

prehistoric something that lived or happened before people began to write things down.

primate any of an order of mammals that includes apes, monkeys, and human beings.

reptile a cold-blooded animal with a backbone, known for its dry, scaly skin.

resin a sticky, yellowish liquid that is given off by certain trees and plants.

saurischia one of two main orders of dinosaurs. Saurischians were dinosaurs with lizard-like hip structures. This order contained a group known as theropods, which were the only meat-eating dinosaurs.

scavenger an animal, such as a vulture, that feeds on dead or decaying matter.

scientific classification a method of identifying and organizing all living things. This method places plants and animals in groups according to similar characteristics. It has seven major breakdowns, including: kingdom, phylum, class, order, family, genus, and species.

sedimentary rock rock formed from weathered products of pre-existing rocks. Sedimentary rocks, such as sandstone or limestone, are known to contain many fossils.

vertebrate having a backbone. The large group known as vertebrates includes fishes, amphibians, reptiles, birds, and mammals.

virus any of a large group of microscopic organisms that live in the cells of another living thing. Viruses are the smallest and simplest of life forms and are a major cause of disease.

warm-blooded having a warm body temperature almost all of the time, regardless of the surrounding temperatures.

INDEX